LIKE A TREE, WALKING

Vahni (Anthony Ezekiel) Capildeo FRSL is a Trinidadian Scottish writer of poetry and non-fiction. Capildeo's eight books and nine pamphlets include *Skin Can Hold* (Carcanet, 2019) and *The Dusty Angel* (Oystercatcher, 2021). Their interests include plurilingualism, traditional masquerade, and multidisciplinary collaboration. They are Writer in Residence and Professor at the University of York, a Visiting Scholar at Pembroke College, Cambridge, and an Honorary Student of Christ Church, Oxford.

T0096533

ALSO BY
VAHNI CAPILDEO
FROM CARCANET

Skin Can Hold (2019)
Venus as a Bear (2018)
Measures of Expatriation (2016)

LIKE A TREE, WALKING

VAHNI CAPILDEO

CARCANET POETRY

First published in Great Britain in 2021 by
Carcanet
Alliance House, 30 Cross Street
Manchester, M2 7AQ
www.carcanet.co.uk

A CIP catalogue record for this book is
available from the British Library.

ISBN 978 1 80017 195 4

Book design by Andrew Latimer
Printed in Great Britain by SRP Ltd, Exeter, Devon

The publisher acknowledges financial
assistance from Arts Council England.

CONTENTS

when i called

like a tree, walking

no metaphor

cause breath to enter

What kept me going was that perfect song I kept hearing,
just beyond the field of perceptible sound.
– JOY HARJO, *Conflict Resolution for Holy Beings*

Where are you going to along rough paths?
– ST AUGUSTINE and HENRY CHADWICK, *Confessions*

For Marina Bartholomew and family,
and i.m. Courtenay Bartholomew

WHEN I CALLED

IN PRAISE OF BIRDS

In praise of high-contrast birds, purple bougainvillea
thicketing the golden oriole.

In praise of civic birds, vultures cleansing the valleys,
hummingbird logos on the tails of propeller planes; in praise
of adaptable birds, the herring gull that demonstrates its
knowledge of how to use a box junction, and seems to want
to cross the road.

In praise of birds eaten by aeroplane engines; in praise of
birds trained to hunt drones; in praise of birds that, having
nothing to do with human processes, crash aeroplanes.

In praise of suicidal birds, brown ground doves forgetful of
wingèdness, in front of cars, slowly crossing the road.

In praise of perse birds like fish smashing out of a bowl.

In praise of talk being cheep, and in praise of men who shut
up about birds.

In praise of birds of death and communication, Garuda
the almost-but-more-than-an-eagle vehicle of the darkly
bejewelled and awfully laughing Lord of Death.

In praise of badly drawn birds.

In praise of white egrets, sitting on mud, hippos, and lines
about old age.

In praise of Old English birds of exile, the gannet's laughter, swathes of remembered seabirds booming and chuckling, the urgent cuckoo blazing on about summer, mournful and mindblowing, driving the sailor over the edge towards impossible targets, scornful of gardens, salty about city life – I can't stand not setting off; far is seldom far enough.

In praise of a turn of good cluck.

In praise of the high-dancing birds carried on the heads of masqueraders and built by wirebenders to carry the spirit of an archipelago of more than seven thousand isles.

In praise of grackles quarrelling on the lawn.

In praise of unbeautiful birds abounding in Old Norse, language of scavenging ravens, thought and memory, a treacherous duo. The giantess down from the mountain complained – I couldn't sleep in a coastal bed because of the yammering of waterfowl. Every morning that blasted seagull wakes me.

In praise of the peacocks invading the car park at the Viking conference in York, warming their spread tails on the bodies of cars.

In praise of the early bird who liberates the dewy worm from glaucous grass.

In praise of birds of timetelling: green-rumped parrots for morning, kiskadees dipping at night: and the absence of birds of timetelling, the unreeled horror of humanly meaningless time.

In praise of the bird of the soul that flies out when the body is molested, and in praise of that bird recalling the abuse room as if perched on the highest point of the pinewood press.
In praise of the blueblack grassquit, which is inky and small. In praise of the albatross, in praise of the double doors to a swimming baths hall.
In praise of birds of concussion, notes in the air being all the brain can cope with.

In praise of birds as edible and in praise of birds as angels and in praise of birds as stones and in praise of Thoth the Ibis.

In praise of the birds of climate change, forest warblers bringing a new song to the suburbs, late-leaving Arctic tern teenagers blizzarding the beach.

In praise of ducking and diving, and without praise of the cruelty of quills.

In praise of birds that are not punctuation, that are not calendars, that are not words.

In praise of birds that occupy and disrupt a lyrical musical staff.

In praise of birds that singing still do shit, shitting ever singing, above a low-rent skylight, on a diet of chips.

In praise of triangulation and three unseen corncrakes by whose calls guests may recognize the way to the house on the tipsy hill.

In praise of increasingly grotesque fossil remains of proto-birds, and the discovery of normality as never having been such.

In praise of birds plucked for dream armour, flame fur, plate plume, and in praise of women who fight like cranes and swans.

In praise of thump and slime.

In praise of fine feathers, prophecies, and export regulations.

In praise of Quetzalcoatl. Tremble to say more.

In praise of the birds of prognostication, gutted, magnetic, or altering their calls.
In praise of rare and less showy doctors refraining from labelling immigrants as insane or aggressive, as more regularly spotted doctors may be observed to do.
In praise of Suibhne, driven mad by the dinning of church bells, yearning for his dinner of unchlorinated cress.
In praise of Suibhne's flights crossing land and water, and Suibhne's poetry crossing time and language, to and from, tidalectic, praise.

PLAGUE POEMS

For Jack Belloli

I. Now We Are Things Invisible

The inessential park is closed.
Its benches clean of homeless
bodies hurting less in sleep.
Cigs, wasteful pansies, gratuitous
marigolds, dogs running like flames
and vaguely sinister statues
are out, like fountains in drought.
The wrong romances will not fall
among its turning leaves. Who'd make
a fearful call, craving escape
from beatings, can't expect to coast
on help from public services.
The sky is roof only to birds
and drones, no place to lose the words
of crazymakers. You can grow
your inward silence indoors now
the inessential park is closed.
Memory restyles it like a scroll,
adding some willows, and a bridge
to which you run, to catch a wish.
The visible, unusable
park; its blue imagined bridge.
For love of things invisible.

II. Plague Fidelity

You may kiss me as much as you
like. I wish you would. I always
wish you would. I wish you always
would. You're the only one allowed
to kiss me. The science is, lack
of touch can make you ill, even
physically. Sometimes when you
breathe, I start breathing just like you.
Do you remember grandmothers,
poems about grandmothers? You
said life's not like that. Could be.
Remember asking, laughing, why
I write – used to – about the sea?
Kiss me. Tell me where you are.

III. Coronavirus Swing

What's different? Why is it different?
Why must we be, when we are not?
I'm beside myself. I'm with you.
For social dancing, read
social distancing. You alone do
I adore. For catastrophe,
read charity. For adventure,
read attentiveness. Oh baby,
I mean it.
                For mask, read ring.

IV. Flowers for the House

There's a tiny lilac flower
with no name I ever could find,
in Trinidad. You'd notice it
at grass level, when you're a child.
If there are pandemic babies –
not like jail babies; they won't spring –
like workhouse babies – lives confined
after pregnancy's confinement –
what are the fairytales we need?
And how to explain about
going Outside? An enlarged heart
in a rocking chair dreams of games
it used to hide from, all the time
all the time also in the world.

V. Ecopoetic Pandemic Logic

What's different? Why is it different?
Why must we be, when we are not?
People push for clear-cut heroes
and heroes' mirrors, enemies.
Who hears an alienating song
in an alienated land?
'We did not kill by bullets
as much as by chemicals
pouring softly into streams
far from cotton T-shirt malls.'
That won't work. Try this:

                        First they came
for the transport. Then they came for
the libraries, the hospitals,

the shelters, the helplines;
they came for your education.
Now they've come for our own good.
Do you agree? For our own good?

TOWARDS AN UNWALKING

After Thomas A. Clark, 'In Praise of Walking'

The Least Possible Baggage is the mother of deviated
ziplocks. O my companion. I implore thee in pink squares.
Dawn alligator-ranges. Apply acupuncture to the frozen
shoulder of this land. I write a card and put it in your
hand and run away. And you reappear before me. Light.
Anticipation.

Violence, Property and Triviality are three sisters. O my
weird. Dance gold into flax, blue flowers into forget-me-nots.
I can begin to walk only if I am also counting them.

To implore the spinning plates of schist, sameway-grained
and splitting. I hold to the nub of the hub, I proceed not,
I halt, this time unmugged, unraped, unstop-and-searchit,
draped upon the curve of Available. Blanket me hard,
unwaged, ungranted. I am not so very plural.

I dream of being a child who dreams of flying.

Take one way out of always. Unscramble the WHY of
everYWHere. For VEin and PatH, read IN and AT.

No creature has been out in it, said the taxidriver of the
printless snow. Snow is a footnote. Footnotes are hotttttttt.

O destination I implore thee not to be detention nor to be
detonation.

Blindfold and touching is another way.

A hive of nerves, an explosion of activity, the apparent waiting of a body in too much pain to walk. O my mother.

He spoke of taking and leaving and the thought sprung unbidden of milk teeth and gold teeth buried between daisies and dandelions in fields.

Please, Dissociation, reveal the gifts the man says lostness brings. Make this the good things called a walk, when the ground peels like a kite caught in the tree I also am, rooted in my own crossroads, unable of any going, no distance from the door to which I have keys.

Ten thousand colours, a million colours, if this road were a slide and hour unawareness a stain, O bacterial terrain of human fallibility.

Recollect a schoolchild collected in a holey car where the felt floor beneath the pedals gave onto the road, gaps for feet if only they could make the running.

Some shun sunshine. Salutations, Shadow, you are my night and day.

Sweet man of the dragonfly T-shirt, how to walk at your light pace? The measure of your poem shadows this noem; doux, doux, I do and I'll do.

Ooh! Lichen it! Moss follow the knowing path!

Leaf it. Just leaf it. Spring green as a crayon drawing on the kerb.

Posh boys do self-dislocation porn. Birdsong mobile apps turn birds away from essential tasks. O technology, O science, O the psychogeographic hims singing for the photoshoot. Posh boys tie no walking boots to overhead lines. Their pronouns are trophied in bramble paragraphs, hard in high-waterstones beauty sleep.

I pray you, earth, to forget falling; precipice, to hold beneath Skye's purple trainers as she rehomes a chenille caterpillar on a frangipani tree; to know Judy's heelstrike as treetops know a skimming owl.

Temporary waterfalls; also, landslides; on the hairpin road to the sea.

~~Uh ah sd & hzclz sd m asthma & sqlsh m leg sd entering thigh-high clay.~~

Nobody walks except vagrants and vendors, she sd, nutsmen and mudmen, up and down the highway; why shd she know how to pee correctly on a slope?

Hell it's an expedition to walk from bed to bedside when you must strap your ankles to feet that can't feel themselves or anything else. Reflex no longer the lex.

Bach is a fish mounted on the howling wall of a moorland pub. Call me sea bass, he obstinated. His wig was as long as this.

If the crown of the ship's mast could break into flower, I pray you, crutches bud; umbrellas blossom; guns branching from the well-trained trees, I don't know what to say.

If you could see yourself. If you could see yourself on the other side of the hill. Slow it down. You're waiting for you. See, there, with a packet of lark's tongue rolls, on the ridge.

A little of the hill crumbled in my hand. The hill is very little now. Rocked in a hammock slung underground, the trees are acting superficially.

Night. Night sets me off.

Dredge me a river.

Night is black and glitter in so far as night's black and glitter glitters back from the river and a goatman's eyes should not be black or littered with pinpoints of gold but if they mock up two of cups twins of the river this is a voided drowning and to look away is to walk over and over to walk over a bridge over and over a bone bridge.

The Walkauthorial's preferred totalities, all and nothing, everywhere and always, are nowhere when the crosser of bridges loses consciousness. Fainting and being pulled up is a tighter and wider form of walking. I implore the return of unnamed abilities to tell stairway from linen and breath from both.

I love my love with a look because they are far-distant. I love my love with a song because their voice is touch. I love my love because they are the weather to this walk.

It's how you incline or buckle during the ups and downs, said outdoorsman Gerard Manley Hopkins to the blades of his ice skates. Meantime, East Anglia sloughed its coastline. Fishermen twinkled for Sylvia Townsend Warner.

This thin bellows coughed blood when it was ten years old. Bubble-trapped, imagination repeatedly got up to go towards its friends. Name ten fluids, secrets, futilities, or secretions blistered into the anonymity of The Walk.

Aah! Run! The pine trees are wading! You cannot outpace them! The gibbet is swinging! Full light of day brings traffic wardens! Aah! Run!

If you can't run, roll. If you can't roll, roll. Role and role.

Poet, will you forgive this imploration of your original, clear air?

LIKE A TREE, WALKING

WALK #2

If you walk slowly,
I'll have further to run.

If nobody has abducted you,
I'll double back to meet you.

By the tulip tree – No.
By the hospital – No.

By where long-ago ladies with flambeaux
sold roast corn and boiled corn,

also No. By the baobab?
By the pretty and stink cannonball tree?

No. No. – You don't walk
very slowly.

Before raper-man corner
and the gingerbread house.

You'll double back and meet me.
A red seed in my hand.
Grey beads round my neck.
You had further to run.

SWEETHEART! IS SO YOU STOP? / CECI N'EST PAS DU CALYPSO

Expanded translations after Pierre de Ronsard

I.

Look this hibiscus blushing like a lover!
Fasten it in your dress nuh, in the part where you heartless.
Take it from me, you ain't play you cruel.
I hover like a hummingbird
You strike me down and pluck me
I hover like a hummingbird
You strike me down and pluck me…
I quiver while you pluck me to make your feather armour.
Look this hibiscus blushing purple like a lover.

II.

Let who want to see, see.
If you want to try, try.
I damn glad
Love's nasty needle stick in my side
fill up with what go kill me.

III.

How you slow so? Lahéing there? Get up!
The own-way kiskadee asking the sky
for light; black grackles, golden orioles,
making a set of noise inside the bush.
The bougainvillea want trimming. The thyme,
the shining-bush, the mint, go dry up,
even the wonder of the world, lilac
and succulent, go dry up, if you don't
get up and take the watering can to them. Girl.
Take the watering can in your little soft hand.

IV.

Run my brain in for sedition.
Hold my soul for treason.
Charge my common sense with violence, fraud and conspiracy.
Death, I want to dead, come and make death with me.

I am on strike from passion.
My love is an industrial action.
I cut off the whole nation electricity.
I am on strike from tender sensation.
I blindfold myself, Love can't baffle me.

V.

Sweetheart! Is so you stop?
Well yes,
turn your back
on the endless commesse.

I woulda even prefer
a cut-eye –
or a cut-tail.
You sometimeish for true.

I shoulda buss a kiss on you.
Like I dotish or what?
My spirit quail up just so.

Is not the new moon
or the green-face man you see.
Doux doux, is me.

This week, the wheel of white-violet days
has been dropping. Velocity burns. Wheel, turn.
The doves have not landed on the roof, no,
their clever feet have not splayed or clung
along the ridges; the red tiles, unpractised
at being scaled, retain heat, while undisturbed.
The doves continue wheeling – I have seen them –
rising like a dust of sublime objection
by the very wealthy or the very young,
able to get up and leave the chamber.
Where will they land, and when? The church has lost
the blue statue from its louvred window,
the shops cleared out their garden furniture,
and toys are sent for by air. Send me then
someplace tiredness must fill my feet, high up,
maybe the abandoned tracking station.
I am no satellite. There is no moon.

HOW SILENCE SURROUNDS

In response to Suzannah V. Evans

Caught or cradled, a crystal globule, a loom of jelly, the
rhythm of anxiety running up and down chords in a tiny
being without anxiety transforms quivering to resonance
adding and adding again to widespread resonance no
body picks up on; submersible bodies being concerned
with floating, thus unaware of the gentle suspensions that
resemble anxiety and are not anxiety, dense bodies becoming
light in gentle suspensions are suffused with a lightened
sense of neither light nor sound. The view is of the sea. A
figure on a bridge far from the sea holds out her arms. The
sun is free to alchemize her sense of inwardness; the sounds
of an entire day, for how many years, until it stopped, no
longer being nameable. Still counting.

WALK #5

Yellow, and black, and pale, and hectic red,
Cling and fall: satin rags from cliffside trees

Each like a corpse within its grave, until
Wrested into resurrection, wrestling

Angels of rain and lightning: there are spread
Nets of wildfire on the charcoal hill

Of vapours, from whose solid atmosphere
Time can't break to run forwards or backwards.

Quivering within the wave's intenser day,
The same striders from changing directions

A heavy weight of hours has chain'd and bow'd.
They pass more often than is possible

And, by the incantation of this verse,
Slot into standstill near the waterfall.

Be through my lips to unawaken'd earth
Magenta petals and an emerald bird,

O Wind! The trumpet of a prophecy
Isn't required. Just bring our seasons home.

STYLISH DEER

Remixed from Iain Crichton Smith, Deer on the High Hills (1962), for Alice

And   three deer   the uniform worms
what it is
     outraged and sniffing
          into the dark wind

know   the ice is breaking   now
great bounding
     leaps like
         the mind of God

return   so return   soldier of the
              practical
walk
  then go
     not

Forget   Ulysses   Hector
And that was death,
     assumption of anguish
         deranged, deranged,

must build   must build from   must build from
              there
a stylish deer
  high hills
     let its leaps be unpredictable

delicate dancers   he shot them   the clean shot did
not disturb
did the deer
                    simply there
                                        simply there

into the live stars   rumours of death   inhabit wild systems
a running natural lustre
                                        tear to indigo
                                                  the fiery guts

Supposing God precarious   bright flesh, sad,
so stand, precarious,
                    beautiful
                                        through your bones

absolute heads   humming in a green place   till later later
later later
                    another head appeared

                                        flashed from his horns,
                                                  a strange cry

wandering senses   [s]mell now the cresses   mortal and moving
unclosing, closing, a bewildering ring

                                        rage of the sap
                                                  in boredom kinship

Deer on the high peaks   a fierce diversity   selves that twist
I am, I am,
            I pray, I pray,
                        inform a chaos

Deer on the high hills all at ease   on a meditative truth
                                                                            impaled
sensuous and swift
                        vigilant always like a tiptoe mind
                                                            on the high
                                                                    hill

Do colours cry?   for the dead?   in inner
                                                                    distances
all the summer day
                        all the stars
                                    the deer, who walk

no metaphor   at random   on an
                                                                    innocent journey
in isolated air
                no other skin
                                lonely is your journey
in isolated air
                dance with a human joy
                                                        the transient journey

WALK #6

Oil painting of itself, this shocking dullness
known to be sea-blue harbour. Paint by numbers.
Sahara dust dumps pink on ochre. Fullness
of allergens. Who breathes in these streets? Cumbered
with a bad job, looking down at his bare feet,
the shamed, outsize angel shakes dust off his heels.
His tunic purple. His task: to spread new plague.

Walk as if your knees are lifting higher,
though it's a gift box shelved inside your chest
that smallens breathing, makes lungs toil. Fit friends crest
eased corners. Red rocks sheer away, desiring
handholds from abseiling vines. So little slows
erosion from extraordinary flows,
hidden water added to explicit rain.

Blue is both an expectation and a thirst
during this climb. Not in the sky. Glossy, rare
police cars midnight past. A cobalt cyclist.
Wildflowers manuals call blue; in truth, they're
lilac. What buildings have those roofs? Where in
Port of Spain? The Gulf of Paria is sundown-
ready, all day, promise of a bluer depth.

The wind blows as he goes about the city.
There's no fixing his hair. Brightness thickens.
People fall. He leans in. Light falls from the air.

CITÉ DE LUMIÈRE / LIGHT SITE

Expanded translations after Eugène Ionesco, Entre la Vie et le Rêve
(Gallimard, 1996 [Belfond, 1966])

I. Alliterative Diamond

Quand j'étais plus jeune, j'avais des réserves lumineuses…
when i was young   when younger i had
light stockpiled   stepwells of luminosity
seams of gleaming   inward glow
brightness had my back   hot buttresses
radiant underpinnings   unreserved reservoirs
my fashion walked sunrays   failings wheeled to sunrise
doing was floating   dear and perpetual
shining went into me   should not go out
look we have resources   my life you have my light

II. Ionesco Perpetual

*[I]l suffit de savoir bien regarder, il faut voir. C'est admirable.
N'importe quoi est merveille, tout est une épiphanie glorieuse, le
moindre objet resplendit…*
Set out for the horizon. Only pack miracles, mirrors and
miracles. Saline vigils may ebb and flow. So that evenings fan
out in laughter, send me night music, via paper boats. The beam
of a lighthouse decommissioned long ago in a world all aglow
stevensons on. Eternity's doing us a favour, see? Selah. Joy to the
hall, whole, moon, lemon, monk, monkey, citrus, parrot, tattooist,
flute-player, nénuphar, water lily, loriot, testimony, surge, fill, fold,
foal, loan, digit, minim, any and every forlorn and delightsome,
what, more… The least little thing is a splendour.

An imaginary holiday
       in a small hot market town
An imaginary stroll
       through some tinkling part of France

An imaginary stall
       with wooden trays of trinkets
An imaginary person
       The sun shines   I can't see

An imaginary doing nothing much
       You like me liking things
An imaginary present
       secondhand   much thought through

An imaginary memory
       a circle nested in a box
An imaginary freedom
       This life is very real

ERASURE AS SHINETHROUGH / L'AMOUR A BESOIN DE RÉALITÉ
After Simone Weil

I. Through

Amour   pas amour   amour
          par le feu   o   God
                    fire

          our   c a l m
Love   o   to rise o   there
    end so   to   love i   s
    s   un   s u   n
    mer   s   u   n
          h   a love   d o ing   be
      ing

II. Within

Amour   in   u s   u s
attach   us   attache   c   ut
    s e coup   e r tache   attach
              cut   us attach   imaginaire
              amour   attache   so attache
    d   g   od   so attach e
                                          d
    c u   t   attached   n   o
rope   entre   entrer
        O   enter   u s   s
et   us   son d e
    a   1   1   e
    very   out   all   var
          i e   s   or   they   or we

41

III. Reality

L'amour   Love   it   i
    s

           loving   lov
       ing?   mort
                M   o r   t
       o   beloved
C'est   m   o   ur i   r
   imagination   is   crime o
     love

NOCTURNE #1

Dogs bark, at least a block away.
The night is quiet, with crickets.
Nobody has fired a gun
tonight, I notice, nobody
within earshot. Bougainvillea
grows purple, grows white, festooning
the fence with spikes. Black paint flakes off
electric gates. Birds have peep peep
pipitted their new calls long since,
the close-of-day chirrups picked up
from alarm systems, not long since,
and now perfected. The city
keeps changing where the district lies,
seldom within its lines. The hill
shows a few lights, more than it had.
The Savannah uncoils with walks
unwalked, during a friend's absence.
I'd fly there now. If I hadn't
eaten so much salt, I'd fly, now.

She stopped in the street and looked up with a conjuring look. Her attention was fixed on me, therefore she was not looking at me; she looked up with a conjuring look. She began to conjure trees. The sky cracked like a white egg. The chapel stood like a cut-out decoration. The street ran like grey cardboard that had got wet.

Suddenly we were in a grove of snow gums. Their trunks were pink like naked ladies, the rosy pink of naked ladies, warm naked ladies holding their towelled breasts while they danced outdoors after a hot bath, several ladies rising rosy out of one and the same bath. Some trees are female in their seeming. Snow gums are female. We were in the street in the middle of a grove surrounded by tall snow gums.

Could you conjure trees? Could you use trees to seduce? Could you look between the standing woman, the lamp post and the chapel and see the impossible pink and white trees? Are we in their sway? She speaks the pink and white impossible. Is it into the here and now?

Snow gum leaves are falling and snowflakes are falling and kissing the air and catching in your hair. We are between seasons and inside both geographies, if this is happening. Are we? We are, if this is happening.

She spoke of trees. She stopped in the street and began to conjure snow gums, but when I looked at her I saw her, the stones were in place, and the air was clear; and she looked at me. We were two people, talking.

Might you have noticed us take our leave and walk away in different directions?

Like you, I must have been on my way somewhere.

NOCTURNE #5

Your number comes up as Unknown.
Blue cat under a car at noon.
Your number comes up on red shoes.
Pas de deux with Señor Unknown
spins you to the brink of blue roads,
red lantana in profusion;
to open and sheltered waters.
You're sure you knew Señor Unknown
as if since the day you were born
till the day he'd pull you aside,
a dance card, a lottery ticket,
a cuneiform bill of lading
with your number on it in his hand.
A kicked jack on the table
for your game of All Ones. Instead,
sometimes he's pulling you closer,
sometimes wandering on ahead.
Sometimes he gives up the tango.
Chants you into his capoeira.
Shows you a Morpho Eugenia
butterfly, makes you think turquoise
while putting pure dark and bitter
criollo cocoa on your tongue.
As if Señor Unknown wants you
to live, preciosa, though he's
no more or less than the open clefs
carved into a violin's curve.
He gestures. You think it's a wave.
Mistake him as beckoning you.

This is a nocturne. Unbecome
the book, Reader. It's way too late.
Unknown – *waves up to two metres*
in open areas – your number
comes up – *but less than one metre* –
Precisó – *in sheltered areas* –
He wants you to live till you're dead.

Told me about a childhood. Running free through rain-
forest. Those were the best days! On all those paths, he
never saw a snake… Told him about a childhood
within walls, snake in the postbox, snakelet unearthed
wriggling, never-seen snake of the drain moving
heavy stones we put to block its resting place. Yard
had the displaced inhabitants of forest… He
would've been running through with his gun and smoke-bright eyes.
Decades and decayeds. *What you see, what you do, what*
you say, what you know, what you believe, what you have
been storying, your self in storage, your storied
self. Decayeds and decades. Is dangerous. Forest
becomes forensics. The frond is dissected. Oh,
it waves over all those paths. Equivocations.
You see? You do? To me? As if I am a wo-
man? Come on. He says. To control. Coming on. He
knows… *Control. You believe. The narrative. What thorns*
mistaken for companions. What canopy. What
shutting out. He discs his eyes. His hooves hurt.

NOCTURNE #6

Night, I'm not going to say
you aren't there. You hurt my eyes
with promises of rest; stretch
weighted blankets on warmed beds
under which the hills can crawl
starring out their masts, mansions,
scars and forests. You press hills
into your dark like a brush
wetting paper with colour.
You are high up and fluid.
Night, I'm going to hold on
to you, today, in daytime
in your absence, in your sharp
absence. In bright fluorescence
I hold to you, surrounded
by fluid darkness, indoors
and out, in scathing sunlight
darkness nonetheless sheathes me
as if I lie down on air,
high up. I have not been schooled
to see like a scientist;
therefore I know your contours
without having to touch you –
and I know you're not there, not
in that way. I am. Body
of exhaustion, frequenting
shops where natural tears are sold
by formula, with droppers;
eyes dried by overwatching,

overweeping – I am not
like that, Night. I expected
to break on you. Holding on.
The time for warning is done,
Night, now is the time for joy.

DARK TIMES MY LOVE

fainting, or pinpoint focus, falling or caught up in sleep –
fragrant, soil-selfish, toxic to felines, loved cultivars
laving your night's noon in saffron and incense as deep
fainting or pinpoint focus, falling or caught up in sleep
washes in gold script washing out only makes brighter, deep
agitation a bee's dance view serene cultivars
fainting or pinpoint focus, falling or caught up in sleep
a garden stays you stay among escaping cultivars

NOCTURNE #7

Happy kilometres, happy sunflowers,
Happy Serpentine Road, Flood Street, Dry River,
Happy gang intervention, happy wedding,
Happy Archbishop, happy oyster vendor,
Happy erased tramline, happy hospital,
Happy office block, happy gingerbread work,
Happy baobab, happy pitch oil rag flambeaux,
Happy gecko alleluia, happy song.

HOLY ISLAND

The wind is high today.

The seals are hiding under rocks.

The seals have gone to the other islands.

Come back this afternoon.

Listen for the seals.

What do they sound like?

They sound like ghosts.

LULLABY #1
For a stormy siesta

rain gurgles more gorgons more
hair spreading snakes in the sky
more mouths drooling infrasong
gutters gurgle dividing
garden into passable
garden and reptile garden.
rest, somewhere a timer says
imaginarily; quakes
won't happen at night, okay,
this timer reassures you;
quakes won't happen during rain,
it lulls; if you let yourself –
okay? – sleep lulled by thunder.

ERASURE AS DRIFT / KINDE YERNINGS

After Dame Julian of Norwich

I. Hazelnut

I   am   ghost   ly

  I   a   m

   cloth   a s   close
    love   as
                              this   littil thing

     in   it

   w   e   d   o   a   h   y   e
s
   ally   *all*   *a*   ll

                    suddenly ha   ll   ow   littil   s
an   d
  my   *love*   *all*

    being   *love*

II. Keeper

littil thing

                                  o   what is

so   l   i
   t   i ll

                          very

  so

    o   a

needy   little   creature   now
              love   how   unmade   is

        a

      so littil

             very

     s   m   all

    why   so l i   t til   thing

       o   love   have

   rest

III. Thyself

        our   full

                                    home

              touching

                                                            art

                      that is less   full

   if   i   want   i
have
all   full   and full er touch
the
             good   good
creatures
and   work   without n   e   e
  d
            only to   stor   e

            bliss   all this   goodness

LULLABY #2

For an unplanned catnap

the lawnmowers are singing Verdi's Requiem
the neighbour isn't laughing or he'd be shooting off his guns

                              tchac tchac tchac kapow!
              those army people KNOW how to throw a fête!

the wind is tossing lions' voices
literal lions' voices

                              ROAR chug chug chug
                              ROAR chug chug
                                      cough

the wind tossing lions' voices
louder than pines

                              I'd laugh like Maurice's piano
                              if I weren't crying, laugh
                              sans gunfire if only
                              not to be crying, why

I'd like to lie down in lilac, lie down like, like
a petrea petal, helicopter lilac
softly onto a grave.

                              Happy the rain softly
                    effacing dates, happy the stonemason
          turning, turning to less dreamful sleep, softly in his grave.

LOVE IN THE TIME OF NEW MEDIA

Voices are beating their wings against glass
in the other room. Sometimes they ask,
'What did he look like?' A hopeless witness,

who can only tell them: 'When he thinks,
his face transforms, as beautiful as daylight.'
Blue and yellow, blue and yellow. Truth blinks

like a child behind a waterfall; scarlet,
the earth turns; the sky stops. They lour. They wait.
'What was your agenda?' 'Wait, what?' Midflight,

a bare-eyed thrush scents fruit; assesses threat.
Will it come here? This room won't quit those rooms.
The witness dreams of an electric gate.

LULLABY #4
For an unfamily chantant Noël

a cello is a chamber full of silk cotton
bow down   alley of lime trees   let my children pass
frightful with   sweetness tilleul   ombrageux unborn
undouen children   pass   you   are the Christmas blossom
laid like guipure on the Savannah you picnic
thoughtfully on   dark red   sorrel, fallen sweat bands,
dark chocolate coated leaf cutter ants   night picks up
flambeaux to stay awake   from you, O my children,
but I tell you, under   every   tree is your space,
under the   grass the   water reservoir   is yours,
your dreams pass lisping into it   when speechmakers
call on ancestors   oh   that isn't you, little ones,
never-was, little   piping ones,   oh   no, you are
the cough in an altar-boy's throat   are   the scrape of shoes
being tied mid-run   come   eat a bench   drink an owl

I'll find you. Where we met. On stone-bright streets
I imagine. We may have lost people,
not ourselves; not yet ourselves. If we have
much to say, we do not say it: we have
had years. A new friend is with us. New friends
are hard to make, in middle age. Who can
introduce us? Silence runs like treacle
over flint; coffee; river water; new
words, like petrichor; green willows, no words.
If this were a sonnet, we could turn. Now
I would turn, and I should have rhymed. I am
without those things they say a poem needs.
Sugar falls off a doughnut in a bag.
In a rose garden. With a pack of cards.

LULLABY #7
For the grieved and glad

Why did I make you wait so long?
Death is a passing state
Night comes late
The nature of a day is long

Strange angers come along
The street breathes us, we breathe the street
Why did I make you wait so long?
Death is a passing state

Sweet whispering
The street wears us, we wear the street
Too living to be late
Too dying to belong
Why did I make you wait so long?

REVOLUTION TIME

Revolution time is a turn
and a turn is a crisis
and maybe how you spell crisis
is where Christ is – maybe not
Revolution time is a turn
about a time not taken
because taken for granted
for given – were you taken
through Revolution Time Wordsearch
looking for LOVE – were you given
EVIL when you wanted to LIVE –
Revolution is not a spell.
Time is now. Time is devalued,
time is monetized, misgendered,
is nothing if not now.
                Time is
revolution you don't see.
Revolution time happening
inside.
                You can't tell by testing
if someone is Revolution
Positive. One-thirty-second
Revolution.
                Who is turning
inwardly? The man cutting grass
turns into a voter. The child
from Venezuela turns into
a Moko. The lady squatting
down the road, you call her crazy,
then you turn a little inward
and call her hungry, take the time

to turn and call her family.
Call her family. I am wrong
in every structure I take down.
Everything we can sing to hope
walls fall, we sing colonially.

Also this. Click off. Also that.
Click off. Revolution time
is reflexion and reflex
action refusing to react.
Revolution time: when you love
to kill your neighbour, but you
click off. Revolution time is
thinking again. Think again.

NO METAPHOR

AFTER AN UNSPEAKING

This is the circus for dead horses only
We are in a tent but there is no outside
                                no breathable outside
There is mud and stars but no ticket-seller
                                and no in-between atmosphere
Somebody uncertainly approaching certainly could not stand up
The mud would suck him down
The stars would suck her up
This is the circus of exclusions, not approximations
The dead horses canter at a soft pace
                                satin around their hooves
The dead horses jump from buckets, landing softly
                                taffeta over the sawdust
This is the trick of assertions without any ground
                                no overlap with anywhere
Your city exists and is unaffected by the circus
                                don't be mean about the ribbons
If they mean nothing to you, they should mean nothing to you
What if the ribbons are in this temporary atmosphere
                                in the only atmosphere
The symbol of grace
But I am breathing sawdust and I cannot see sawdust
                                and my pockets are full of receipts
But twigs are clinging to my clothes and the tent-pole is not a tree
                                leaves are on my shoulders like expired tickets
And I am fond of horses, even these ones grinning without stopping...
How did you get here? You did very well to get in
We have to muffle their hooves. They might have to cross a frozen river
Hooves muffled as if with eastern basketwork , yes eastern
                                enclosed horses
                                far-distant horses

I was in an airport and a man said it was all about him
He was the colour of a number of ladies' perfume boxes
                         duty-free, rosy with broken veins
He was lyrical, it was only him and the girl behind the counter
His instant love went into a box and into another box and into
                         would you guess it
A third box
But by the final couplet he was alone again
His solitude took up all the lounging space in the airport
                         paid and free
And none of the security cameras, only the girl's insecurity non-cameras
Occupied themselves with him
Throughout the numerous terminals
Ignorable special gift displays, his timeless well-stacked gift replay
And one thing I surely can tell you
This is what romance looks like and you had better review it
                         in print
For throughout the numerous terminals
                         he was innumerably unpolitical
He was a poet and worked as a poet and this is how poetry works:
                         the girl answered him blushingly
                         perplexed in all the right ways
I don't have her training, I don't know what she said
I don't take your word for her lines or that I no longer resemble
My passport photograph
                         potentially unpoetic
                         actually a serious problem
By now he's in a magazine as well as being in a faster queue
                         pearling along without price
                         almost but not quite beyond purchase
Would you ransom him perfect-bound
                         does she have his digits
You would be right to call me bitter but I don't care
That the female security guard is feeling up my tights

Electric blue and black stripes, my foot on a stool like a little bucket
So long as there's a café on the other side
                    I don't care
My I.D. is uncertain but like a certain kind of poet I want caffeine
                        nothing has killed my want of caffeine
Bring me a horse as well, why not, I am ancestrally out for stars

What was wonderful was to find war could involve neither death nor waiting
Because everyone was long dead and in translation
Still I dare not inform the prophetess that she is no more
A series of epithets, no more than a series of epithets
                        with her burning hair
                        she eats time like air
And never looked forward to being in a poem
So long dead, so often in translation
                        as not to be political
I suppose she did look forward to being history
Which is not the same, cantering at a soft pace
Which is not the same, reaching down for the stars in a sky-facing bucket
                        tented over
                        void-filled to the rim
I wanted at least a blanket to give her in this cold and quilted circus
But she already was holding out the purple veil she kept for spare
And I had given away my sword, a real-life event
                        best left without record
For so long its curvature had been my security though now I hold
                        to other things
And couldn't prove what was gone, having no proof in my possession
No proof of the bird-head hilt and sharp curve as ever in my possession
                        and it was the wrong kind of sword
The trick of disappearing was neither hers nor mine
                        only words
For to point out what isn't there in a gently textiled circus
                        is political if ever under review
A good review at minimum three days' work, how beautiful
                        without pay

This is why please do not mention the ocean except as bluegreen
Whaleroad swanroad path of exile only for domesday-booked living bone
                              excise such crossing times as might be political
You must see it without the wrong ships in mind because
The ocean in a poem must not become political
                              and further
                              bluepurple
It is unfortunate your friend's book was political before it was born
Because of where he was born
                              some places are political
Also his body thunders politics, let it remain dark in text
                              some bodies are political
From their conception
                              let them not imaginatively conceive
Though you know nobody brighter in love
In the camp as in the city, across the sea and across the desert
                              no prizes for loving
We feel his love launched as if the political were personal
But haven't your missiles already landed?
How is your personal not political?
                              free and spacious
                              fine and small
Your poetry has the biggest free trade deal the world has ever known
                              unilateral and non-reciprocal
I am tuned in and hearing you musically the while you refuse to know

When Fay Weldon's team came up with the slogan
'Go to work on an egg', did the Holy Spirit move them?
When some underling did the drapery for the luxury photograph
And leftover children at the hairdresser glimpsed infinity in the purple waves
Who dare say the Holy Spirit did not move them?
Why are you bringing the Holy Spirit into this?
I didn't and if you did, I didn't understand you
I understand you didn't mean me to do this after you
                              didn't bring, didn't dare bring…

As most people reading wouldn't
                              wouldn't believe
Far less advertise the Holy Spirit
                              like Duane Dove's fine flavour chocolate
                              or a bar of Dove soap
And the signpainter who ought to have died but persists
In embarrassing and luckily undocumented environments
Shakes involuntarily in every part of his body except his brush-hand
And the typographer who is much too young and persists
In collecting the signpainter's art for never-to-be-commercialized fonts
Is too close to the edge of the forest and too far into the city
To be a true artist. This is not true
Art. Make no mistake. True art
                              is otherwise
And on the curriculum and not without citation
And has a studio without needing a studio
                              nor dreams of demanding a studio
And the curriculum from which this poet learnt is cancelled
By time passing
                              and now not without citation
Don't touch me
                              this is no kind of office
Even if I walk to the lighthouse I only walk to the lighthouse
You have a card that opens the way to the river
The way to the river is closed
                              I don't have a card
Some movements are truer and more co-operative than others
Just look how
                              I've lost form

WINDRUSH REFLECTIONS

I. Windrush Lineage

They came in earlier ships,
Mahadai's ancestors and mine,
with hope, and by imperialist design;
and I am too young to have seen them
dying, as she says, on streets.
I am resigned to dreaming them
wherever Victorian iron
palisades the public squares
like spears. I take her word
that the bread they died wanting
was British; the languages
and laws denied them were British,
for a quarter of the globe
rose pink to cry empire,
havoc, and natural resource.
    This was recent.
Recent enough: my cousin
saw them too. The finish
of those ships overlapping
as ships ineluctably do
with others, keening the curled
wake with a forward-looking wave.
    The sea is like this.
What you expect nobody
can expect. What you accept
nobody can't accept.
What the great hungry puzzle
stamped with a crown is

must be big enough to see
big enough to ignore.
   Why wouldn't you
take a canoe, a pirogue,
carrack, caravel, ocean
liner, yacht, banana boat,
naval destroyer, oil tanker
or cruise ship, why wouldn't you?
When survival becomes
an acquired taste, improvement
a second skin, and home
is a long-distance love affair
with loss, and home is an arranged
marriage to glorious, unseen London?
   Windrush wasn't the first.
The voyage was not an arrow
flying one way to lodge in sorrow.
Island people met island
people on the docks. Some were there
long time. Some stayed. Some went back.
Twelve to a room, cold in welcome,
post-war Britain already was home
by birthright: documentation
was not a prize or a promise
for this generation born under
the far-fetched Union Jack. Citizens
drilled in the hymns and nursery rhymes,
sweepings of a dust-devil map?
Singer, soldier, fabric designer,
novelist, nurse, BBC presenter,
stowaway, activist, carnival maker,
lawyer, bus driver, self-reinventor,
brought up as British in sightline and grip
crossing to Britain, the way some move

to Leeds from York. Surely. Sure. No more.
   Sugar brickwork, tobacco boulevards
and bloody wool are the well-known parts
making Albion's very groundsong
a subclass of Caribbean harmonies.
   It takes a special effort
to tune out the transatlantic
jumbie jumble ripple
in the Humber and the Thames.
Hear now: Lord Beginner. Lord
Kitchener. Sam Selvon. V.S. Naipaul.
Mikey Smith, stoned to death in Jamaica.
Una Marson, ruling the airwaves.
Wilson Harris. The nationality
act in one of its ever-revisable
revisions. And a prime minister,
and a journalist…

II. Windrush Caribbean Cento

Things does have a way of fixing themselves.
Cyaan mek blood out a stone.
Be it enacted by the King's most Excellent Majesty,
one grim winter evening, when it had a kind of uneasiness about London;
by and with the advice of the Lords Spiritual and Temporal, and Commons,
fury and diamond.
Is a place where everyone is your enemy and your friend,
or else like charcoal to grain.
An Act to make provision for British nationality.
I am glad to know my Mother Country.
Rest, then, my heart, thou knowest but too well
I an I alone.
Where I come from you take what you want

and you pay every Friday,
and for citizenship of the United Kingdom and Colonies.
But let me just look at what the policy…
Cricket lovely Cricket!
But I keep coming back to it:
Your hostile environment policy.
The compliant environment policy,
The government is taking action against
every person who under this Act is a citizen of the United Kingdom
and Colonies,
a dancing dwarf on the tarmac.
Spirit of leaves like smoke.
A burning injustice.
But our hearts are white.
A burning injustice.
But their hearts are black.
God is sen you His spirit,
Windrush.
This lady died.
Because the English people are very much sociable,
every person born within the United Kingdom and Colonies,
in the womb of converted horse
in the Christmas supplement of the colour magazine,
you're absolutely right,
shall be a citizen of the United Kingdom and Colonies by birth,
but as me gon in
cock-roach rat and scorpion also come in.
What is it that a city have
that any place in the world have…
room dem a rent.
Hate dat ironed hair.
He looked in the mirror one day
and couldn't see himself.
Citizenship by birth.

Citizenship by descent.
Citizenship by registration.
After all was said and done,
Birth is never treason.
And he began to scream.
You thinking about the thing without a name
You get so much to like it
you wouldn't leave it for anywhere else,
subject to the provisions of this section.
Second Test and the West Indies won.

III. Windrush Exhibition

I fail the bag check. Once in,
my phone falls under suspicion.
It feels like pulling a string
when I give the names and the reason
that let me photograph the exhibition:
Songs of a Strange Land.
     There are no arrows. You make
your own way; excavate
your own gates. What is a keeper?
     The 1700s names and sale prices
for old to underage slaves
sold off with a Tobago estate…
But that is not Windrush 1948?
The footage of 2000s Brits driven out
for a retroactive lack of paperwork…
Is all Caribbean heritage Windrush?
     I miss the delight and taxonomy
of birds, woods, foods, medals or geology,
the ocean of non-human
lapping humanity.
     But here are voices

beyond glass cases: letters
between brothers, entertainments
in community magazines,
funerals and arrivals,
achievements, doubts and designs.
   If only 'shock and awe' were a phrase
we could reclaim, not to mean 'war',
that might lift off with love, like good labels do.
   Can these stories, their satin and skulls,
good-clothes and cologne, like a Pierrot pun
or a Robber cloak, unfold unfurl unfall
their particular nuance, universal burn,
300km away as the egret flies
from London to south Leeds?
   It is not informational, it is
not a blameshift, it is not
all-lives-matter top down and sideways blank.
It is in itself important,
crucial in the crucible of history:
these isles and these isles
these shelves and these selves
these aisles and desires
these disasters and out of disasters
these stars and the astronomer out for stars...
If you could send a postcard
to the past, send a postcard
to the future, if you could
welcome, warn, object or anything else
that reaches flying, what would you, would you,
if you could, would you send, would you have
sent? You on the journeys from Ireland,
Bangladesh, Cumbria, you with different
literacies, you in the forest
of skilled restoration, achievements by your hand

and unsigned, you with the quick eye to sketch,
you on the everlasting buses?
You share your music and tell me
you'd take a calypsonian to lunch…

IV. Windrush Leeds Cento

Stay, if you've come all this way.
I also know about uprooting.
In the airport the smells were
mixed. Anxious. Friends
to lonely, what a journey.
Who did you leave behind?
Approach. Anxious. Someone
to love. A travel buddy.
You will be welcome here;
we finally settled.
How was the voyage?
Come here! I would
take you for a walk
and show you York. Leeds
Town Hall. Kirkgate Market.
Bradford. Chapeltown. Spain.
Blackpool. Windermere. Turkey.
Not everybody lives in Buckingham Palace.
I'd like to show you round
Leeds. Celebrate the NHS.
Dear Mr Churchill… Dear President
Kennedy… Getting experience
after unemployment. Nursing and tending
to old soldiers. Can't wait for peace
and quiet. In this big freezer.

Family near me.
Know the area. Explore. Enjoy.
I walk around the park
and I found a friend.
Please sing another song.

IN PRAISE OF TREES

I. Moss to Mozart

The fire tree is now a moss tree. The leaves which had it standing in a pool of fire have dropped and not been cleared. Assimilated into silt, they make mud of the road. The tree stands in its own delta.

Moss clumps on its torso, way past the main fork.

Moss covers every side of the tree except the east side, which could be mistaken for the north.

More traffic arrives from the west. More pedestrians arrive from the east. The traffic brakes for the lights. The pedestrians talk about walking. I search for birds which become unimaginable.

The lichen is numerous-fingered. If I could have translated piano practice into botany, the lichen is that Mozart phrase my left hand trialled endlessly. The lichen is in A major.

II. First Person Arboreal

The fire tree picked out in its leaflessness by sodium lighting looks like things other people may not have seen: frozen waterfalls in winter, jets of water frozen by strobe lighting. It is pale and I am tired. I lean against it and close my eyes.

Before hearing the sounds far away from us, I must forget the sounds I made getting here; the bough I kicked, the creak of my coat, my feet in the mulch of dropped fire. I close my eyes and listen as if I were looking. Sound will not perform like sight. A road to the south roars like a curve. A road to the north roars stop-start. I feel quite sick. Solitary runners clomp and make awkward diversions around us, bigger than needed just for the tree, for my humanness – not my size – makes the tree bigger. We are obstacle.

How much of what I expect from hearing is touch! The cold wind flips and ripples my hair across my forehead, and it feels like it should be a sound. I fool myself that I am hearing the hedge. It is tinnitus mingling with traffic in a small bay between my left ear and the tree trunk.

I feel you while I hear me as only you allow.

III. They Go Quiet

The marriage tree makes a noise. It has a thick body. When I walk up to the marriage tree, the wind drops. It's as if all the trees I want to visit in stillness equally want to partake of silence. On this site, dreadfully smug engines whoosh and hoop, regulating the temperature of prohibitive buildings, pushing out the traffic to go drown itself. I used to work here.

Leafy footsteps, light with purpose, one Working Late person at a time, cut through from my left, to my right. My eyes are closed. I am thickly canopied by the marriage tree, even if its leaves are not rustling, even if its roots are pooled in concrete and its body is hedged about so I cannot touch its bark. Skeletal clanks from my left and to my right: bicycles being unlocked.

I want to pretend I hear leaves. I do not. I want to stretch my arms crosswise, as the footsteps and clanking proceed right and left. I do not. I leave hearing a little sound of my coat about my neck. I leave knowing how, when I walked up to the marriage tree, the leaves rustled.

IV. Egrimony to Embrace

The avenue of trees revisited in memory is closed off by gated compounds the size of citadels. For more than two hours I walked widening and narrowing circuits of their alleys and by-ways, always checked by a wall or a gate. I see where the long-desired avenue must be, across the black river; though not exactly. I make a rollcall of distinguished men who, at a knock, might be surprised into kindness. Their names and silvery bodies might let me through the stone courts that control the much greater expanse of dark green slopes leading to water. I think with bitterness of famous poets of the recent past and the unasking present: men who could say, "Let me through. My eyes enrich your vista and my words make clear your water." Instead of trying words, when my body will have forespoken me, I walk around the access points, following through to their locked inevitabilities; walk over bridges, espying climbing places, aware of surveillance technology that renders quest into criminality; I lock eyes with an all-weather old man standing guard in archaic garb, who seems to know that I am up to something, and I decide to spare him the trouble of doing his job. I gave up on the avenue and did no wrong.

So much noise in my head when the clump of trees arrests me. It is severally woven, hence its ability to hammock a hemisphere of sound, soughing at a height.

Still the traffic and bitter musings mess about in my head.

Bicycles ease over the bridge.

I am positioned like someone about to jump, in order to share the clump of trees' stillness. There is water between us.

If riders notice, and when walkers pass, we are nothing worth stopping for.

I break into nervousness. Not yet present to the clump of trees, I am afraid of not finding them again. Not much distinguishes them. I count lamp posts. I refer the clump of trees to other, more distant treelines; I hope to match up significant shapes, but night is brushing off oversignificance of any detail. I imagine inviting a quiet friend, anxiously, to this place, and not finding it at once. I was eager for trees; and frustrated. I must be careful about exciting another eagerness I cannot satisfy.

Gradually the road traffic becomes a milky ribbon, east and west. Gradually the bridge traffic becomes a flow to which my back is turned. Neither stream of traffic sound borders me in any way that constitutes my borders. Gradually the clump of trees assumes me. There is front sound and back stillness. They do their thing. I lean in.

V. Tree of Approximation

Listening to a tree with another person, listening with a tree to another person; listening or hearing? Who conducts attention to the rim of the sky? Start there. Start twice, and that is twice again.

This time the thick canopy of the marriage tree is rustling. My ears welcome and embrace the sound. It slips down much closer in hearing than sight would have allowed it to reach from the curve of leaves above. My eyes have closed, you see. My heart is thudding; my body knows that, not by sound. Small plants were trembling; I remember them, but they do not add in their small sounds. Footfalls one way and a single dry leaf the other way do skater tricks of sound, up and off from the ground, more volume in the air than you would think from looking at them.

More than you would think. From looking at them. We love. This tree.

VI. Intentionally Wolf-Inclusive

It is raining when I hurry to seek out the clump of trees. My coat is made of a loud material. As I move through the dark streets – it is not yet nighttime by the clock – rainfall hits the coat, loudly, from enough different directions as to make it seem that the rain is approaching from different heights. I am a percussive mess when I get to the bridge. None of the student body dotted about with and without bicycles, lingering in virus-friendly groups, makes a sound of noticing; none interrupts the sound of their commingled murmuring, when I climb onto the railings, lean over the scummy river, ignore the glisten, and listen for the trees.

I am listening with the trees.

Rain hits the water from enough different directions as to make it seem that the water is approachable from different heights. Rain is being shaken off the black weave of coniferous branches. I cannot pretend to hear it. I can only pretend to hear it.

I think myself into the further reaches of the weave, then move closer to the clump of trees. I do hear droplets. My attention shakes off the clank and gossip of the bridge. Awareness branches all over my coat, and in the drumskin hollow of my ears, very lightly, hitting and rolling away again.

I am a musical instrument of the trees, and it is raining.

VII. Flashback to Belfast

There is no way of being shocking that shocks. An artist's shock is an expected delivery. Ready to be absorbers, the consumers of art; they're hyper-absorbent. You know what is shocking? Care. Care is shocking. Attention is shocking. Being soft and slow. Radical care is the new revolutionary. Forgive me, for I have sloganized in the café, where my colleagues long ago reconciled kindness and subtlety. (This is happening before the plague.) My present colleague sits flaming quietly with tenderness and the students, like so many New Year lamps, bend and flicker inwards. We are sitting in warmth.

There followed (in a colder city, water between island and island), during the permitted exercise of lockdown, six instances of stillness with trees. You don't hear in order to listen. You listen in order to hear. Start with the furthest. Name, note, move on. Move in. You are hearing your own interior, yes, even the mindbuzz randomizer, even the bodyshameful procedures. You are not hearing interiority to the exclusion of anything else. Your interior soundscape becomes audible in relation to everything else. Surround sound is a condition of surround silence.

I station myself by particular trees, and start.

CAUSE BREATH TO ENTER

FOR WHOM THE MOON

What is a moon, what is a mind,
what is a man, an area of darkness,
what is a mare, a getaway,
what is an astronaut, he carries out
instructions, obedient and armoured fœtus
whose woven and worn lunar tether
could be any hiker's failsafe terracotta
litter, if not returned to preserve with glass care
a memory few will ever have and some still say
didn't happen.
          O tell us –
earth of breathable fabric, earth of eyes,
          O tell us who we will not –
earth of spontaneous colour, earth of fools,
          O tell us who we will not send,
unquenchable earth, to the moon...

*

O tell us who we will and will not send,
discworld earth, to the moon,
          to land
in the Sea of Tranquillity, to be saddled
with names from a science faulted with wonder,
as if there were seas on the moon, thirst
for seas that are states of mind, the sea of
Moscow also a state of mind?
          Send
nobody who'll run mad across the sand,
no nightmare hippy wet behind the ears
looking for blooming moonflowers, burrowing

moonpups, moon roos boxing at the edge of
overly silver pools.
                        Send
the fair to middling housekeepers
who don't fix their clothes after they put them on
to go out, who are better at mending than ironing.
Kudos to the hoisters of flags with wrinkles,
showing the stars the stars, the overreached
symbol, the possible infinity
                        we can begin to count...

poets you spoke like stones in water / going against the grain /
wearying and refreshing / what you gain / in true reflection is
reflected in lost income / that was then / and since then what we
learnt / is truth must feel hard and must be a process / violent
triage / when did it start / have you applied your skills to that /
or are you still above origins / violent triage / between the violet
/ and varied green / did it slip past your guard / flashing fake i.d.
/ modelled after pleasure-pain? / check in with me / check up
on me / interrogate me like nobody interrogated me / caress me
in an agreed fashion / transfer the xmas list to an excel sheet /
excavate this for me / violent triage / did it start with a game /
seedhead fluff / blow that / love friendship hate marry adore /
cross out the letters of your classmates' names to get results! / is a
buzzfeed quiz the acute phase of / the soft face of / violent triage
/ congratulations your colour is indigo / check out your soulmates
who are indigo too / when did you aspire to be spiritual / but
not religious? / before or after supersize duty free three for two
chocolate bars / relaxed you and revved you up / for online dating
/ the mysterious appeal of stranger danger / big data is just the
boy next door / when were you / complicated in public? / before
or after you began withholding / coins from beggars who had that
look / or that look / who is the heroin in this case / violent triage /
help them by not helping / and are you a soft summer or a bright
spring?

i was writing a poem with dogs running / & i wanted to
distinguish them / the curled one / the deep-chested / the ridge-
runner / a poem with dogs running after their master / a hunter
who turned into a deer / but i couldn't / finish / violent triage /
have you ever recanted a poem / this puts you in the percentage

of people who / the doorbell was ringing / the downstairs american
oxford neighbours / wanted to check / by chatting on the intercom
/ if i was doing terrorism / i was doing transcriptions / have you any
idea / whether those are citizens beside you on the bus / she wasn't
even baptized but she declared for catholic / which saint then / it
just kills me / poets / do you live near water / or how many footsteps
away / and how many footsteps in a day / do you take towards water
/ it is advisable but not enforceable / to throw stones / this will
raise the volume / unless you are in the situation / of which child
for school which for the cotton harvest / testing times / but do you
think we could ever / be like that?

violent triage / do you have smart goals / scared / measurable /
achievable / reproductive / televisual / violent triage / whether in
pastel / rose-gold /or electric blue / is viral in our minds / crowning
that other virus / natural / to ask / who is dead / who's as good as
/ violent triage / plan accordingly / did Google translate you / as
disponible / or disposable / cross yourself when you pass a burial
ground / what about when you see / a smartphone / but you were
indigo / you can't be expected to see cobalt / did Google translate
you / as available / or valuable / bow your head when you pass a
cemetery / but you have venus in aquarius and are more likely to
keep it cool / let me do your chart / let me pull a card / violent triage
/ dream of a tidy resurrection / because the angels can't be left wing /
from rows of graves we'll pop / like municipal tulips / don't imagine
they'll rise up then / citizens of everywhere / the vast unmarked /
in what eschatology does death lead to decolonization / the sea will
push up too many timbered heads / violent triage / stories of how it
all ends / what is the critical faculty / what kind of sickness / we all
suffer from / something / violent triage /a new poetics / silence of
the heart

ODYSSEY RESPONSE

I. Words, take wing

Words, take wing, fly commonly among all people
who have power of health and employment over us;
go like the sparrows rife on summer streets of a holy
island; unlearn any fear; flitting, bring to mind
light, and how quickly light fades; bring to mind life,
comfort in houses, fragile as windows onto space.
Words, take wing, as if lawyers were angels, as if death
were a paper doll in a set of identical
paper dolls, an infinite set of paper doll kings
of terror, cancelled by a gentle fiery sword.
Sometimes, words, you launch in many lovely languages; yet,
before you begin to fly, you are misrecognized,
like an owl entering a superstitious person's
open-plan room being beaten to death, Athena's
wise bird struck down, bloody feathers everywhere,
a soft body a futile piñata
releasing clouds. Could you gather up a faith
in strangers, in the absence of a god of strangers?
Does any homeless person gleam like a god in disguise?
Disgust rules. Do without. Doing without big symbols.
Zeus! Eagles may acquire cruel associations.
Words, take wing, fly commonly among all people
who share vulnerability on a trembling earth;
who drink, or hope to drink, sweetly, cool water.

II. Hero?

Tell me how to simplify a song. Tell me about
identity; fidelity. Solve the problem of a face.
Tell me about a state governed by emotion – would you move?
Choose to move? If they force you into moving?
If you cannot afford to, cannot afford not to –
Make a song about one person. Who can cope.
       Is it a hero you want? Why not say so?
I am suspicious of heroes. How do they survive?
I know a mother who scattered her children
on the way out of war, and has not gone back to look.
What if the hero shining like a falcon arrives
having traded their body for life, trailing killings
and transactional sex? Is the hero empowered
to treat their spouse to raw cuts of trauma, treat them worse
and better than anyone else? Help can be a trap.
Home, a mating of traps. Who do you want at your back?
Enough. I am privileged to have civil conversations
in a corrected city, commemorate the correct dead.
       How changeable is a hero, like modern rainfall patterns.
How fearful is a hero, patched like an archaic sail.
How lifted up is a hero, like the great-grandchild
of immigrants, hurting his parents, hoping his child is kind.
Witness those ghosts who, after a natural disaster, don't know
they're dead; poor, wet ghosts, trying to board real taxis home.

III. The sea

Hooves, chevrons, arrowheads, champion ski racers, nothing, no,
nothing runs so swiftly, nothing seems to run so, so
swiftly as cool water pours back in, making
an island of a piece of land once, sometimes, no more
than another part of the shore, a tidal island.
Nothing runs so swiftly. Did you think I was singing
about death? Should we give death preferential treatment?
Should we be women singing to death? You saw. You know.
The sea is a cover for bones, how busyness covers news.
New bodies are laid every day in the innocence
of the sea. New burdens explode every day
in the innocence of the air. How many
of my family dropped like shining falcons
in the duress of a forced migration, ivorying
into the sunken halls of the only Atlantis
really worthy of the name? The sea is a cover.
There is a law of the sea – No. The sea is lawless. –
There is a modern law of the sea. The conference
proceeded for nine years. – No. It is a convention
of the toothless, for the toothless, by the toothless. The sea needs
teeth. – How can there be freedom of the sea without protection? –
How can you be territorial about the sea?
Most of the civilized – America never agreed. Never –

IV. Companion

I tremble to think of meeting you. How did we meet
on this trembling earth?
   A blizzard blew up. We sat
on a stone, a few paces from the farmhouse.
We could not see, or move, to go to them. They could not
come to us. We could not discern the tide, rising towards us.
   How did we meet?
   He had turned his back on you. I loved
the poetry of your anger. I wanted the poetry
of your anger on my small island. Transported. Cherished.
Forget any other kind of kiss.
   I tremble to think of not meeting you. You could be
better off. Light was fading quickly. You saw. You knew
I was unsafe, waiting, in my full-passported femaleness
in the cruel associations of a village
of privileged abandonment. You sat on the bench,
reached beyond death into Persia at your back,
unrolled for me a mat of pure imagination,
placed for us both a vase of pure imagination.
Your metamorphosis was from refugee to host.
In the street, you gathered guest-right, offered me
hospitality where had been others' hostility, till
my neglectful, official friend arrived. We thrived, like two birds
in an embroidery orchard of pomegranates, oranges,
and weeping pears: like impossibilities of climate
redemption.
   They spin epic words to say none of this is home.

V. Hades Social

Be thankful for the friends in a blue and white country
who invite you to meet their dead. Together, in a small group,
crossing the clean-smelling river pierced by mossy rocks,
enter among tombs like garden sheds, houses;
graves with lost names, granite pitted by acid rainfall patterns.
Rub flowerless hands over lost names. – Try not to bring
anyone home with you, someone invisible says
in your memory, sharpening into many voices,
women singing to death.
        What is this place? How did you get here?
You know. Graveyards are unclean. The only way to go
is by fire open to the sky, on fragrant woods,
white camphor tucked under your tongue, releasing spirit
from the ragged body to the innocence of air.
– I cannot be burnt, I cannot burn as I need to
burn, among these new friends, these kind friends, thinks the stranger.
Be glad to meet the new kind dead your friends have buried. You saw.
Next time bring flowers. – But I am sad for my future,
in a country where my funeral customs are illegal.
Whose problem is a soul? Identity? Fidelity? Death
is a thief in a stationery shop. He strolls out.
The shopkeeper, a poor man, runs after, shouting. – I saw you!
Give that back! – Give back what? Death says, strolling out.
Hermes is a tram attendant who holds your coffee,
helping you find the coin you dropped; it rolls underfoot.

VI. The faces of Odysseus

When the trembling earth dips away from our common ancestor,
a wife living as a widow may look at the streaks and stripes
of another seaside sunset, beauty in isolation,
and tremble like the earth at the men lined up
to land on her like shining falcons, quickly, but not lightly.
If an old person perseveres in life, yet needing your care,
do not harass or tease them as Odysseus did,
tricking his father into hardworking tears, washing his brain
with real grief and reactive gladness.
You know, you see Christ in the face of a wounded enemy,
if you listen to the now-celebrated poets weeping.
What if you hear the song of yourself simplified on the news?
What if your song is impermissible as the blacked-out news?
Odysseus, I see you. I know I thought I might
dislike you. You were so hot. You planned it: standing naked, hot,
in the doorway, drawing the long bow no-one else could.
Standing where Penelope could see the slaughter of fine men
her hero would commit, war for an indoor Helen.
I see you in the face of the vagrant thoughtfully
washing his clothes at the standpipe in the Savannah
under the trees with no-one to care. No-one, Odysseus.
One man's soldier is another man's beggar, Odysseus.
He lives without love or teasing, sweet talk or complication.
One woman's king is another woman's case, Odysseus.

VII. Zeus, god of strangers

Stranger, how are you cast away, cast upon your own
resources, cast on wildly different styles of hosting?
What if your angry host feeds you up to go to war?
What if the gifts lavished on you lay expectations on you
to go away, make a success of yourself, and don't come back?
What if you are blown back, empty-handed? You would be
right to hide your name. Yes? You are a king at home. No?
Slaughter and laughter cross your threshold
in your absence. Slaughter and laughter at a distance
shadow and echo you, no matter how you set off,
or your clean presentation, now, among the élite. Yes? No?
Where are you? Islands aren't always islands. All maps are pop-up.
Volcanos yawn, spatter out something the sea covers over.
Rivers rise, or silt up. Clumps form, or dissolve, barely the size
for two blue-coated Norsemen to duel on.
Islands are provisional. World; whirl. The sea covers over.
The Queen of the Dead lifts, in her lily hand
with its violet nails, a head of snakehair.
Do not go too deep. That way paralysis. You want action,
like tired people do. Stranger, you are cast like in a dream
of being on stage, unprepared. Is it right to invent lines?
Traveller in body, buffeted about as a guest, Zeus
loves us. Spirit Traveller, revive as a good host. By Zeus,
Time Traveller, if you see Columbus, shoot on sight.

VIII. That's epic

There is a city beneath the city beneath the city
beneath the floodplain. Forget about it. A city
is at the back of the city at the back of the city.
Ignore it. Ignore the scripts in which mathematics
and astronomy were first written. Ignore the scripts
incised in rock, the scripts inscribed in landscape.
O Muse, make the poet move on. Memory is no good
to triumphant civilizations.
O Muse, your poet is blind, saying life has a sheen.
O Muse, your poet's a hostage, saying land has a meaning.
Nobody likes a try-hard, a lacemaker working
with a vascular surgeon to join delicate gaps.
Put memory in the service of intention
to keep the story shining, like tears shed over onionskin,
or the cheering faces of the well-fed family watching
screensful of migrants plummeting or washed up
at a border, from a wall. The camera admires
guards, themselves descended from migrants.
The shining chorus of weaponry,
made manifest by taxes, drops death
on more children shining and their many lovely languages
as if they were done for from the get-go, like paper brochures
in a digital age. Forget about it.
Keep going. A story has the tricks of appetite.

ACKNOWLEDGEMENTS

First published in *Odyssey Calling* (Sad Press, 2020): 'Holy Island' appeared in *Cambridge Literary Review* 12 (2020). 'In Praise of Birds' is a response to the memory of improvising for Caroline Bergvall's 'Conference (After Sweeney)' at the International Literary Festival in Dublin (May 2019). 'Odyssey Response' was commissioned by the actor Christopher Kent and pianist Gamal Khamis for their narrative recital *Odyssey – words and music of finding home*, premiered in November 2019. 'Windrush Reflections' was commissioned by Poet in the City and the British Library for Collections in Verse. A response to *Windrush: Songs in a Strange Land* and the communities of South Leeds. Inspiration for 'Windrush Lineage': Mahadai Das, *A Leaf in His Ear: Selected Poems* (Leeds: Peepal Tree Press, 2010). Sources for 'Caribbean Cento': collage of Lord Kitchener; Lord Beginner; British Nationality Act 1948; Andrew Marr and Theresa May, 30/09/2018 interview, BBC transcript; Wilson Harris; Una Marson; V.S. Naipaul; Samuel Selvon; Michael Smith. Sources for 'Windrush Leeds Cento': collage of original material by participants in events in Leeds. Thanks to Jo Lindsay Walton and Samantha Walton of Sad Press.

First published in *Light Site* (Periplum, 2020): 'Cité de Lumière: Light Site' was written for Zoë Skoulding, for inclusion in *English: Journal of the English Association*, spring 2020. 'Sweetheart! Is So You Stop?' was originally published in an earlier version in 2020 by Roof Books in the volume *Queenzenglish.mp3: poetry | philosophy | performativity*, edited by Kyoo Lee, containing short pieces by 50 writers from around the world on the topic of standards in writing and their effect on freedom of expression and creativity. *QE3* focuses on the diversity of the English language in transition, conversing with the world of dynamic "Englishing" and its polyphonic futurity. Sources: Pierre de Ronsard, 'Pren ceste rose aimable comme toy', 'Quand je te voy seule assise à par-toy', 'Qui voudra voir comme un Dieu me surmonte', in *Premier livre des Amours* (1552) ; 'Marie, levez-vous, ma jeune paresseuse', in *Second livre des Amours* (1556); 'Ode sapphique XXX', in *Poésies diverses* (1587). Thanks to Anthony Caleshu of Periplum Poetry.

From *The Dusty Angel* (Oystercatcher, 2021), a pamphlet of twenty-one walks, nocturnes and lullabies: Walks #1, #2, and #3 and Lullabies #1, #2, and #3 appear online in *Anthropocene Poetry* https://www.anthropocenepoetry.org/post/3-poems-by-vahni-capildeo Thanks to Charlie Baylis. Nocturne #4, Nocturne #5, and Nocturne #6 appear in print in *anthropocene everyday: sensibilities of the present* (Dostoyevsky Wannabe, 2020), ed. by Maria Sledmere and Rhian Williams. Thanks to the editors. Walk #5 is a 'coupling', a form invented by Karen McCarthy Woolf, which pairs a line of found text with an original line. The italicized lines in this coupling are from Percy Bysshe Shelley's 'Ode to the West Wind'. Thanks to Peter Hughes of Oystercatcher Press, and to John Whale and the University of Leeds poets for their sensitive critique.

'For Whom the Moon' was written for and appears in *Giant Steps: Fifty poets reflect on the Apollo 11 moon landing and beyond* (Canberra: Recent Work Press, 2019), edited by Paul Munden and Shane Strange. 'How Silence Surrounds' was written in response to Suzannah V. Evans, for Chris Turnbull's collaborative project, *If/Then*. 'Love in the Time of New Media' was written for and appears in *No News: 90 Poets Reflect on a Unique BBC Newscast* (Canberra: Recent Work Press, 2020), edited by Paul Munden, Alvin Pang and Shane Strange.

'Revolution Time' was commissioned and a performance filmed for the virtual edition of the Bocas Litfest 2020. 'Stylish Deer' was written for Alice Meyer's session in *Mænads of Necessity*, a collective spring ritual undertaken during my Judith E. Wilson Fellowship at the University of Cambridge. 'Towards an Unwalking' was written for 'Imploring the Territory: taking the language for an unwalk', a performance, Q&A, and interactive workshop with Polly Atkin and Harry Giles at the Scottish Poetry Library (July 3 2019), and is part of a collaborative, limited-edition flipbook. Thanks to *Cordite*, *Plumwood Magazine*, and any other publications that may feature or have featured elements of this book.

Source for 'Erasure as Shinethrough / L'Amour a Besoin de Réalité': Simone Weil, *La pesanteur et la grâce* (1947). Note on the text: erasure of a bilingual interlinear literal translation (French/English). Source for 'Erasure as Drift / Kinde Yernings': Crampton, Georgia Ronan, ed., *The Shewings of Julian of Norwich* (TEAMS Middle English Text Series. Kalamazoo, Michigan: Medieval Institute Publications, 1994.)

Thanks to the University of York, where I am Writer in Residence. Thanks also to the Seamus Heaney Centre, Queen's University Belfast and to the University of the West Indies, St Augustine, for hosting me in 2019/2020. Lasting gratitude to friends including Polly Atkin, Jack Belloli, Emma Bolland and Brian Lewis, Mary Anne Clark and Dominic Leonard, Harry Josephine Giles, Skye Hernandez, Iain Morrison, Ron Nevett, Elena Fiddian-Qasmiyeh and Yousif Qasmiyeh, Nat Raha, Judy Raymond, Annie Rutherford, Hanna Tuulikki, Colin Waters, Fr Dominic White O.P., J.L. Williams, and Lydia Wilson.